INVENTORY OF DOUBTS

LANDON GODFREY

TUPELO PRESS

NORTH ADAMS, MASSACHUSETTS

Previous winners of the Dorset Prize for Poetry

Jesse Lee Kercheval *America,
that island off the coast of France*
Selected by Ilya Kaminsky

Mario Chard *Land of Fire*
Selected by Robert Pinsky

Thomas Centollela *Almost Human*
Selected by Edward Hirsch

Lauren Camp *One Hundred Hungers*
Selected by David Wohjan

Maggie Smith
The Well Speaks of Its Own Poison
Selected by Kimiko Hahn

Jeffrey Harrison *Into Daylight*
Selected by Thomas Sleigh

Ruth Ellen Kocher *domina Un/Blued*
Selected by Lynn Emanuel

Rusty Morrison *After Urgency*
Selected by Jane Hirschfield

Joshua Corey *Severance Songs*
Selected by Ilya Kaminsky

G.C. Waldrep, *Archicembolo*
Selected by C.D. Wright

Sandra Meek, *Biogeography*
Selected by Jeffrey Levine

David McCombs, *Dismal Rock*
Selected by Linda Gregerson

Amaud Jamaul Johnson, *Red Summer*
Selected by Carl Phillips

Rachel Contreni Flynn *Ice, Mouth, Song*
Selected by Stephen Dunn

Ilya Kaminsky *Dancing in Odessa*
Selected by Eleanor Wilner

ISBN-13: 978-1-946482-53-2
Library of Congress Cataloging-in-Publication
LCCN 2021023936
Classification: LCC PS3607.O325 I58 2021 | DDC 811/.6—dc23
LC record available at https://lccn.loc.gov/2021023936

Cover and text design by Howard Klein.

Cover art: "Successive stages of grinding a stone egg.
[Imperial Lapidary Works, Ekaterinburg]"
Sergeï Prokudin-Gorskiï (1863-1944), photographer
Prokudin-Gorskiï photograph collection,
Library of Congress, Prints and Photographs Division

First paperback edition November 2021.

Tupelo Press
P.O. Box 1767
North Adams, Massachusetts 01247
(413) 664-9611 / Fax: (413) 664-9711
editor@tupelopress.org / www.tupelopress.org

Tupelo Press is an award-winning independent literary press that publishes fine fiction, non-fiction, and poetry in books that are a joy to hold as well as read. Tupelo Press is a registered 501(c)(3) non-profit organization, and we rely on public support to carry out our mission of publishing extraordinary work that may be outside the realm of the large commercial publishers. Financial donations are welcome and are tax deductible.

maybe i should have wanted less.
maybe i should have ignored the bowl in me
burning to be filled.
maybe i should have wanted less.

—Lucille Clifton

Contents

Afghan

Very loyal to individuals, blankets object to being used as metaphors for vast declarations. Each time a blanket covers a body, it tries to keep the dusty soul alive through the night. With what devices? Stripes, satin trim, a pattern pricked out in embroidery floss, weft, warp. While it's true that occasionally a reprobate in the ranks rises up and denounces the entire enterprise of singular devotion, even that blanket can't claim for sure truth holds eternal value. As it exposes a body to dangers seething under the bed by uncovering a toe or an entire foot, the rogue blanket could feel a twinge of remorse. Just don't say anything to it about all regrets or all terrors, all oceans or all hearts, those abacuses tallying away in their ichorous accounting offices, offering false assurances to everybody.

Atoms

When the antique inkwell arrives after making the journey from its dead owner's estate, the other objects in the atomic ranch house observe it with cool attitudes. Clearly, they think, those curves and etched filigrees bespeak an affection for philosophy or power. Therefore, they shun the inkwell, keeping their own straight lines and unadorned exteriors to themselves. What they never guess: the lonely inkwell is illiterate. Only the masterful sterling silver pen can read.

Attic

Where shall I hide my things?
—EMILY DICKINSON

The attic: separated for eternity from its twin, the basement. Architects and their congregations segregate root vegetables from boxes of tintypes and the board games of children who've moved away. There's a fur coat biding time in the attic too, made with the pelt of a mammal that would be extinct if not grown to be worn. All the other animals we don't like to garment are dying out. Maybe termites will destroy the attic. Then we wouldn't have to listen to roof ridges squeegeeing smudges off the sky's magnificent blue window.

Aviatrix

She sits between two men who touch her arms with their arms
a steward drops multiple things on one coffee stirrers ice a sugar
packet in his crotch the other man's cowboy hat says he'll kill you
on a dusty road when she falls asleep the plane falls in fact the
plane is always falling and the engines work hard to keep it aloft
and the coffee service is always falling too and the violent man
chews his banana gum and the smell falls and he and his violence
fall and fall one way or another the ground will meet us all

Biter

He's a biter, repeated the host. Late summer sun oozing through Houston and pouring in Palladian windows, glowing the beast. An older woman in pearls said, *No, really?* A younger woman in pearls agreed, *But he's so cute.* Too close to her, my lover said, *Believe it*, even though everything he said sounded invented on the spot. His money, jaw, hair, posture, and the hair, the hair eradicated precedents. All of his history seemed slightly implausible, because he wasn't so much born in Akron or on Park Avenue as he was forged in a heavy collective fantasy. A mix of Adam Smith doctrine and movie magazines. To look at him and see perfection was to further harden the chitin of societal norms. This is the shell we built together—now drag it around.

Boa

Like a benevolent queen, the armoire loves all her inhabitants. So when a shoplifted pair of grey trousers starts to boast and question the street cred of other clothing bought with money earned by labor, counted by accountants, and remunerated by management, the armoire reminds everyone there's no telling what cruel whim of fashion's about to rule the world. *I know a pink feather boa that could tell you some weep-sad stories. Put it this way: one minute you're drinking Manhattans and talking to Warhol, the next you're hoping to be anywhere but a thrift store on October 31st about to be laughed at and stained with fake blood.*

Boulder

Unable to fit in anyone's pocket, a jealous boulder considers cures for loneliness while it pauses on a cliff.

The phrase *churchless infinity* will try to mean something to me during my hike today. I will ignore it, distracted by a pebble in my shoe. Nor will I hear what's next. But, in my own defense, it is very difficult to hear silence.

Box

To relegate a box to servitude, one must cut away three sides and call it a bench. To please a box, one could fill it with stones. To practice indifference to boxes, one can merely keep walking past that stranger's mansion without ever wondering about the missing thing keeping someone inside awake all night. But impeccable indifference is elusive, and you must not be discouraged if you don't achieve it at first.

Bush

I'd just moved to California and was driving on the 101 surrounded
by thousands of cars pouring toward the Valley like lava from a
profligate volcano. At noon on a searing Tuesday by the side of
an LA highway, I saw a bush burning. I didn't stop. No one did.

Ceiling

The floor's doppelgänger, blueprint of ideal space.

A dream of nothing.

Champagne

I am buying eggs and tomatoes and lettuce and bleu cheese and North Carolina bacon and apricot juice and a chicken and two bottles of champagne and the cashier asks about them I tell her this wine's the original champagne that it was created by monks it tastes nice and dry the 86-year-old bagger whose birthday's Monday and who will not be celebrating he'll be going to get some cord wood from his sister in South Carolina starts to describe to the cashier how I'll drink the wine in a small glass I will pour it after smelling the cork I will stick out my pinky and take sips fancy and dainty he says he doesn't have wine in his house just MD 20/20 my mad dog days are over I say which prompts him to imagine my five houses and two cars and he's naming more things while wrapping the champagne in individual brown paper bags I walk away from his fantasy of my life I walk away he's either flirting with me or he hates me so often impossible to tell in the mountain's bruised shadow

Cigarette

You are eighteen. You are back in your parents' house for the summer. You are smoking in bed because you've been in college a year. You light your bed on fire. The fire is an accident. The bed was constructed in 1801. You wonder when the mattress was made as you pour water on the fire. The burnt mattress cover reveals a pile of hand-teased horse hair. You know this is not the only creature that will suffer for you. You hear the horses in the barn snorting and stamping in the cold night. A boy gave you the green-leather-covered lighter on the nightstand. He stole it. You light another cigarette. You don't worry about getting in trouble. No one noticed when you burnt the rug in your room playing with your chemistry set years before. Dawn will be as cold as midnight again. These are not warm fires.

Circus

At dawn, when the sun rides its unicycle across my eyes, a silent circus movie has tented and sawdusted the insomniac television. A ringmaster's perverse jodhpurs abuse the tutu of a dewy aerialist. She can't go on. *No, no, no*, a title card whimpers, worrying the oblivions between player piano notes. But here comes the hero! A bowler-hatted man in a too-tight coat balances verve and bad luck on the high wire, while three monkeys bite his nose and pull down the man's baggy pants. Savior! Waking as that girl, I sing morning praises from the little black hymnal of your moustache.

Crumpled Paper

A roughed-up cloud of manual energy—hands cupping, exerting pressure, strangling the flat, the smooth, the pristine—no, not a cloud, a planet.

Cy Twombly *Untitled*

Wordless elegance of gesture, white ovoids strung on grey ground, asking with radical politeness that we consider surface. So we do, standing in cool museum air, in the unerring illumination delivered by magisterial skylights. All day the painting reminding everyone of a chalkboard, rare universal artifact of what we call civilization. When we turn to leave, graffitied prayer (O Void!) performs last rites on our visit. We're more alone now than ever.

Diet

A woman decides to lose weight she drinks only milk and eats saltines she feeds the same food to her dogs books pillows mirrors shoes the house gets only water it is very fat they all become thin but the house looks terrible its windows sag in their frames and the roof droops the shingles are flabby the house craves spaghetti pork chops wine the woman relents and gives it some milk in one version of the story the house discovers unknown joy in the appreciation of simple taste in another the house burns itself to the ground its last meal all the water in the well its last ecstatic vision milk extinguishing a candle

Dishrag

Dreaming of the ball gown it will never be, the dishrag rubs another plate dry and catches some missed oil in its waffle-woven hem, its private fastidiousness violated. Once a crown of cotton bolls, it had pulled sunlight from the sky like royalty receiving gifts from a foreign dignitary. Now the dishrag experiments with justice, releasing some moisture back into the freedom of the air, while retaining a few drops of water indefinitely in a grease-guarded cell. The prisoners will never be charged with a crime but will eventually be pardoned by scissors that cut the rag into scraps destined to polish furniture into beaming monuments of class stratification.

Dog

It takes a long time but a dog teaches himself how to
read he goes to the library he sniffs marrow in the old
hexameters and urine blood bile feces gold dreams clog
histories full of gourmet odors the dog is happy but
tells no one having also developed a preference for the
anonymity of fur an endless purity threatened only by
his aspiration to modesty

Dog

A man says his dachshund, obviously in pain and noisily so, fakes injuries for sympathy. Her cries extend the horizon of her back, and the owner of the suffering animal refuses even a postcard view of this blazing sunset. We can begin to make some preliminary notes towards a maxim about anthropomorphism: If a dog cries out in pain, it is a dog. If a dog snuggles you, then it is more human. But any creature can fake love. Which is a form of pain. So maybe the man was right.

Drawing

I draw a champagne coupe using a fine-tip black magic marker, horizontal line midway through the widest part of the bowl indicating the meniscus. Circles = bubbles. Later I'll find a colored pencil and infuse the drawing with golden soul. Because this drink exists as a cartoon, some yellow circles will float forever above the glass, eternal delight.

Elephant

Let's have drinks, shall we? It's such a nice day. We're civilized
people after all. The lawyer just sent a nice bottle of bourbon.
Small-batch stuff from a place in Kentucky that used to be

a still in the woods.   I imagine that's
actually the case   for most distilleries.
Did you know that   *Appalachia* isn't
pronounced with a   long *a* sound? *Appa-*
lat-chia. Appa-bat-   *chia. Appa-cat-chia.*
Appa-shut-your-   *trap-chia.* Oh, look.

The ice bucket's full. Isn't that one of the great pleasures in life?
One finds ice right when one needs it? The Mona Lisa, penicillin,
an ice bucket filled by unseen hands—how lovely life can be.
How something de la something. Well, let's have drinks, shall we?

Entropy

The moment before the glass hits the tile floor, it remembers with pleasure how well it carried water, how exquisite water looked framed by facets and the tall tapered glass of the glass itself. Always unable to decide if it was composed of walls or one continuous wall, the glass spent most of its time in the cupboard reveling in how specifically it presented the separation between inside and outside. It had liked least being stacked on or under other glasses, having its interior used as anything other than a vessel. *Oh! for another moment of vesselness*, the glass thinks. Meanwhile, the tile floor's beside itself with excitement. Almost never does it get to smash something into such small pieces that a few glass shards will elude broom and vacuum, to wait patiently for proffered vulnerabilities.

Execution

They lowered a bucket of mussels down to my stomach where a table had been set with white cloth and a single candle. My starred beret drank a glass of champagne though it preferred water. Whoever is afraid of silence will never hear it. I see night leaning on the sun. I see a tree leaning on an axe.

Feet

Feet love no one, not even themselves. They demand the most expensive shoes and then object when asked to go to the post office. They beg to be seen at the disco, then don't want to dance. They'd prefer to flirt and play footsie and get drunk. The feet don't love you. If you ask their philosophy, they say something stupid about Mecca or Calvary. Feet obviously didn't pay attention in history class—they tapped out a Morse Code of impatience all their years in school. Just wait till they're old. They'll start spouting ideas from fifty years ago. Suddenly toe cleavage is slutty. But look at their photo albums full of low-cut shoe vamps. Beware the advancing political conservatism of feet. When the generals come, you might want something other than fuzzy slippers to run in.

First Date

*Open wide and let me in,
or else I'll set your world on fire,
but you pretend that you don't hear.*
—A1

a pun : the washing machine :: outside agitator : inside :: we talk :
animals do more things with their mouths than we do :: the bird
on the cottage roof sounding one thing over and over : a wooden
ball dropping in a wooden box or the bird picking up a wooden
ball :: how fur and blood on tarmacadam : roadkill :: how the
bird picks up bits of flesh : how a car bomb exploding next to a
library could horrify :: hat old hat warm : someone making saffron
rice tonight even though her husband's out of work :: neighbor
shutting the air shaft window because her husband died in a fac-
tory fire or a forest fire : how turning away changes to follow and
follow :: a lit match near a wooden ball : our universe reduced to
toothpick-scale model :: universe complete and incomprehensible
: amid the flames a ringing phone an open door a bed

Flame

Flame burns only one temperature, gasses the grill pitchman on TV. Many stars would disagree. That one last night that smoldered blue above our lake talked about the whole panoply of hots and colds. Small blond dog sleeping on lap. Jet fuel. A Vermont lake's deep dream of idyllic love. I don't know. So many people want to be right, I almost never need to give an answer. But if I were to solve for x, I'd include the glacial slowness we sometimes feel when we try to catch up with the horizon. And the green-ball-and-brown-stick trees we drew there as children. Those trees stuck straight up out of the flawed lines we—with such crayoned exactitude—placed right in the middle of the page. My hand trembled. Your hand trembled.

Floor

The wood floor looks up at the rug blanketing its face and wish-
es it were reading a map, an old *Pravda* spread open on public
display, a billboard warning tourists against bear-baiting shows,
something besides the same Bakhtiari garden pattern day after
day. The rug wishes it weren't being followed.

Fox

Like all foxes before him, he shows his teeth every morning and practices his death-speech: *I long to take you under a bush, where we can talk about the moon and candies we've never tasted and theories of adoration while a cool breeze tickles our buttocks, and all the universe sings to us and only us for one exquisite moment its tender song of lust and grief, foretelling my mouth around your neck and your panic followed by surrender, significant only to you, yet know this: you will give sustenance to a world of maggots and small things of a scope and variety you cannot even imagine, a universe of lights as bright as our own despite its absence of laureates to praise the necessary industry of dismantling the world's bodies quitted by souls on their way to new surroundings*, but, like all foxes before him, the fox never gets the chance to charm any victims because surprise remains his weapon and not eloquence, so for maximum symbolic effect and some panache in, let's face it, an otherwise bloodscrabble world, the fox brandishes that delicious bushy red tail, a flame scintillating for a split second in our long dark.

Glue

No substitute for confession: letting a thin layer of glue dry on one's hand and then peeling it off. Though the subsequent palm ghost moans so pleasingly about freedom from sin.

Hemlock

An immense hemlock bullying a little house does not know that tomorrow four woodsmen will chainsaw and chip it into logs and dust. The wood boards siding the house have tried to warn the tree. Not listening, the hemlock blames everyone but itself.

Hemlock

The morning after an immense hemlock's cut down, light fills our cottage living room through a once-blocked window as if a murderer has ungripped a throat. The window feels such happiness that now it wishes it were bigger. Daydreams fill the window with a vision of Victorian greenhouses. So much glass. So much permission. The window says to itself, *Thresh. Hold.* But our little dog lives in the room and can't see any squirrels without the hemlock. The long day inside grows longer, like a mountain of rubber tires burning from now on.

Houseguest

I once thought: Oh, God.
I want to live in every house.

—Esther Freud

Stained throw pillows crowd you on the sofa with friendly obsti-
nacy like someone else's old aunt repeating a long story at a party
you didn't want to attend. A one-hundred-year-old wool blanket
spreads out its stripes on the bed like biotech crops planted where
an ancient forest has been felled. And when you try to sleep, the
house whispers like a guillotine blade on a business trip cooing
reassurances to the impatient basket below: *Back soon, Darling.*

Husband

One evening after he comes home from work, the sun has moved on from our house. The windows can't see the forest, which now hides behind the sky's chalkboard. A box of strike-anywhere matches waits by the wood stove like a gang of extras in a vendetta movie. Instead of dragging it against the stone floor, he lights a match on a windowpane, the little flame looking out into the dark forest. I did not know it was possible to force fire out of the interaction between a small chemical-tipped baton and the smooth transparent membrane that says of course you may keep imagining outside and inside won't ever collapse into each other. I thought the surfaces of both parties in the exchange had to be noticeably rough. Not a miracle, but this new fire feels like one for a moment.

Ice Bucket

I sing to you of special decades and the gullible among you believe
you've missed parties given by moonbeams trysts in coat closets
with fedoras and dancing with wisps of shimmying fringe or fast
cars sailing magically through four-way stop signs without harm
I shake a few melting ice cubes and somehow you forget blood
hocked jewelry leg irons divorce sanitariums bodies hanging in trees
limbs in ditches bullets in walls heads hearts don't worry there's
still time for you to ruin everything at the end of the night you
and I are the same: vessels holding warm liquid temporarily

Ice Cube

Like the unknown handsome Black actor who bravely tells his
military confrères to stay frosty when xenomorphic aliens invade
the ship hurtling through space in this year's groundbreaking
film that changes nothing, the ice cube will be the first to die.
Persuading liquor to stay calm or convincing some aromatized
wine to keep its wild herb notes quiet—dangerous work. Bourbon
smokes a cigar, or wormwood wine tells a nostalgic story about
a meadow in France, while the ice cube tries to hold on. Maybe
another ice cube will join the fray. But instead the word *deliquesce*
slips in, liquiding, melting away to *de-ice*, not abandoning its final
sibilant gesture until the last se—

Insomnia

Cradling a head, a down pillow says it's stuffed with all the incarcerated feathers' memories of how the firmament feels. And turning & tossing the head says, *I'm crammed with this body's thwarted desire to fly.* The pillow says, *I am the attic of the bed.* And the head says, *You wouldn't know it, but I am the basement of the body.*

Inventory

To fall out of love—is to see instead of him,
a table, a chair.
—Marina Tsvetaeva

this is my glass of water and this my jar of water these are the weeds I'm calling flowers this is my piece of bread this is the egg I'll eat for breakfast and this is the tomato I'll eat for lunch this is one of my walls this is my window this is the bit of outside that freezes on the inside glass this is the fireplace the logs the hod the woodpile in the snow this is my coat this is my chair I have paper and pencils this is a blanket with three stripes red yellow blue this is a silver bowl this is the silver bowl's tarnish this is my silver fork I use it every day no tarnish I can't tell you what this thing is it doesn't have a name and I don't want to give it one this is my silence

Jackal

How the jackal eats the elephant anus-first, like entering a castle through the tool shed.

How more jackals will follow the first inside the elephant.

How the stunned elephant is trying to die but is still alive each time the video plays.

How someone is watching that video for the second time.

How night fomented infrared technology and this invention: a small green jackal approaching a large green elephant in a black rectangle.

How the video is playing now, the computer screen abattoiring a dark room with knives of light.

Jar

The jar can't remember what it carried into the house—a quart of honey maybe. Now flowers shatter from spice to stench in its competence. Today an ample pink rose has started to rot. The jar doesn't know how to help. It has always been plain. But more and more the jar wonders if anyone's ever going to remove those last few clots of label glue. Trapped water heckles the glue from inside the jar. The rose drops its handkerchief. No one picks it up.

Joke

Do I miss our running joke about being brainwashed by the Diffi-Cult? Dressed in the ascetic garb of our high school teachers—brown corduroy suit with high-water trousers or brown woolen A-line skirt, brown turtleneck sweater, flat gladiator sandals laced to the knee—one falls in love, engages in arguments about the meaning of endlessness vs. the meaninglessness of endlessness—adding the double-suffix *-lessness* to everything: everythinglessness—bangs one's head against the wall instead of chiming a gong, walks through streets paved with books, envies that American movie star who, in her twenties, couldn't tell a TV interviewer where she'd been to high school—enviable erasure! In the Diffi-Cult, one remembers everything—especially the unattainable rememberlessness.

Junk Drawer

After I die, please let your new wife throw this detritus away. Allow these things to become holes in your heart's blanket. I promise you won't need my rubber bands, extra buttons to the ratty cardigans I wore around when cooking gardening reading that you'll have given to a charity shop, tags from my pied dog lost in Vermont so many summers ago, local merchants' logo-screaming magnets I wouldn't let you put on the refrigerator, the odd champagne cork, notes about errands I either did or didn't do, and the rest of it, all the flotsam and jetsam from the ocean of moments we weren't paying attention to because like everyone else we thought this world would last forever. Let your wife change the drawer liner and lay in her own provisions for the duration, until such time as this little kitchen-corner-tucked coffin's opened for the next viewing.

Kettle

Various as dogs, kettles live in solitude. A kettle's celibacy contributes an air of desperation to its priapism, though the kettle generally succeeds in its water-spleening goals, expulsion after expulsion. Because it rarely bathes, the kettle endures as a hero to terrified minerals, who prefer grouping themselves together in colonies, building structures that invite the very deportation violence they fear.

Ladle

The most generous of all utensils, perpetually giving. Before its career as a saint, the ladle was a bowl, begging for food, begging for drink. One day a handle grew up from the sides of its alms-for-me attitude. At first the ladle resisted this new life of emptiness. It clanged against the side of pots. Later gracefulness appeared in its dipping and pouring method, which, like all forms of ballet, exemplified stringent ideas about civilization. Tamed, pious, it no longer flinched if someone drank from its side rather than waiting for proper service. Now the ladle pities the mouth, a savage bowl always waiting to be filled.

Lampshade

When you say, *I told myself I wouldn't cry*, I imagine you giving the order, *No Tears*. Your denial of tenderness could be the opening salvo of a greeting card with which you share a lack of knowledge about what's valuable. The old woman wearing the shabby black cashmere coat who refuses to ride another train ever again, the father whose well has gone dry—he wanted to own land even if in a desert neighborhood—they carry a few tear-shaped pebbles in their shoes. If my light bulb had the right wattage, I could shine those stones into faceted diamonds or prayers to that deaf god you keep calling God.

Light

The wild golden giant does geometry lessons using windows as tools to create parallelograms, and a small mutt, who must stay inside a cold apartment alone every day, sits in a patch of sunlight feeling like a respected king basking in glory, though he must move every so often because the giant abandons premises over and over as a dutiful show of faith in universal reality, which the dog wouldn't choose to believe in unless he were offered a biscuit.

Luv

You are an expense account minibar and an unopened can of tennis balls. You are a sick bag still folded neatly in the airplane seat pocket, air conditioning lowered to 65 or heat raised to 73, attendant-pumped gas, a McMansion great room, catalogue-bought seashells, a designer t-shirt scored at a discount store and a convict-cleaned highway median, an electronic cigarette, free overnight shipping and free gift with purchase and trans-fat-free margarine, 0% interest, year-round clementines, discreet Botox, a cell tower shaped like a palm tree, and multiple DVD players installed in a minivan. You are the first few rungs of a Ponzi scheme. You are the euro. Beer in a screw-top aluminum can, GMO corn, a viral video of teacup Chihuahua puppies sneezing, a smart phone, and an auto-tuned pop hit at #1. But, Darling™, you are also that quiet just after the stainless steel refrigerator cycles off, when momentary emptiness blesses everything.

Magsolia

*A something
overtakes the
mind—*
—Emily Dickinson

So. So look at the teacup magsolia blossom, unshadowing on its skeletal bough, a so inviting hand dawn-partnered and so ready to twirl onto the dance floor, dipping the light so far back we see exposed throat and cleavage, light's oblivious pink-slippered foot pointing to the so bluer and bluer ceiling. So you can stay so unhappy watching and rename the months like Nasoleon did so—so now it's Desirium, so you know disoppointment will fill the pockets of your sleep with tree frogs that have so no sense of what you like to hear in a night melody. So on either side of your doubts, the external acoustic business of your ears circles around noise culverts, indiscriminately admitting so ugly somphonies, so new words, so ideas you so don't want. In this field you've sown for yoursolf.

Marriage

Marriage, our problem solving system, transforms stale breath, stuffed blue recycling bags, soap slivers, and internet porn into stale bags of internet soap, stuffed blue breath, and recycling porn. Look at those split wet candy wrappers. If the problem solving system recognizes danger, it asks, *Will you act like your mother or father? Will you smoke cigars for breakfast, fuck your secretary, buy ten new pairs of shoes and redecorate the living room again, unzip that other man's pants while admiring your manicure?* The problem solving system can make you wear a toupee, hostage your children or dog, stuff your secretary slivers into a stale bag of porn breath, smoke the unzipped living room of admiration, manicure your secretary danger, dog your hostages, and children your mother and father into a pair of blue candy cigars, your ten new toupees redecorating the breakfast soap or fucking the internet dog in another man's pants. The problem solving system problems your system solving till you recycle smoke, till you breakfast on secretary, porn a toupee, candy a split—till you're unzipped by death, that wet wrapper.

Mezuzah

A woman hangs a cage in a doorway. No bird. The woman sings.
In the distance something in the sky. Bird? Thunder? In the cage
a parchment that is not a bird whispers. No sky. In the distance
something in the distance. Many no birds and many no clouds?
In the cage a thunder. In the woman a doorway.

Mirror

A deep hole in the wall. An empty well. An excavation. Terrible memory. Every face a surprise. Every time. The ornate frame, half of a long marriage, tells the mirror the same stories over and over, the mirror eager to hear them, but to its depthless mind, repeated stories always sound new. Beautiful but old, could have been silvered just yesterday for all it can remember. So it says. Hidden in the lustrous shine of endless light, the mirror keeps a secret: no lover's completely unlike another.

Museum

RANDALL HUFBAUER, 1965-1990

your paintings ghost-glazed and suspended in the museum of
memoryfactured beauty paintings shy like new deer among bare
trees nub-antlered yet crowned by visions of chandeliers swaying
dark above their heads why didn't you wait for those candles to
light my cold eyes want to put on your black coat your black coat
hanging in the forest's closet my eyes like beggars in the winter
with gloveless hands full of snow and you saying *eat the snow*

Music Criticism

Twang they.
—GWENDOLYN BROOKS

Lonely, the dead do their best to entice. They purvey their secrets like department store clerks waving perfume cards. They yell at your dog, stomp around, snore. But ants drown out all that opulent sound jingling the spare change in their pockets. How noisy, the dirt.

Needle

An agent from the Bureau of Pain asks a recruit, *Would you rather sew patches of old patterned fabric together to make remember-burdened quilts, your point sharpened every time you rest in a sand-filled pin cushion, or stitch up a wound, pulling thick night-black thread through tender flesh, securing raw blood edge to raw blood edge, you and your crux used once and thrown away?* Chopsticks and pool cues have all the luck, the needle thinks before answering.

Night

I live in a house that loves me.

—BELL HOOKS

I drive through a forest at night. The trees offer their hands, like dancing partners. I want to say yes, but monogamy pulls me home. That shared solitude makes the bed with flannel grocery lists in the winter and in the summer, sheets that sail along lantern-lit coastlines. The moon tonight swears it's never been to a party. With the pride of a hermit refusing post-Iron Age technology, the moon face-washes with the rags of tree leaves before going to bed. Outside the forest a village claims—and I believe—it too has never been to a party. Maybe someday someone will give the houses new dresses and play the fiddle for them. Looking for home in the somber basement of the day, I tell my pyjamas it won't be long now. But so far away they can't hear me.

Obituary

once dirt sitting shiva in a rectangular hole once a sable brush
loaded with vermillion dragged through wet fuchsia paint then
centuries later a museum visitor asking is he caressing her and the
curator saying no he's stabbing her once dirt hiding its face in the
hole dirt praying to be fired and glazed to bear water wine some-
thing other than that girl then everyone she knew then everyone

Pileated Woodpecker

Named for pileum's red crest, jaunty hat-haunted crown bird
bossing the boreal forest with every *cuk cuk cuk*. Logcocking holes
into pine trunks, pin-precision pickaxing scars into bark. Snag
& jag: feast & nest. Cavities drilled, quit, abandoned. Leaving
dwellings for squirrel, bat, wren. But sheltering snake, this bird
abets an enemy. Common mistake.

Poet

After the reading last night, I was walking the visiting poet to the hip restaurant for the requisite group dinner and by mistake took him much farther. We'd just met and were talking—not so much gossiping as much as bonding—about a mutual poet friend whom we both love but who hurts our American hearts with his superior Eastern European morals about sex. Later when the visiting poet mentioned him again and said, *Our friend will be upset we did it,* the entire table laughed and wondered *what and how much and when and what and what and what* had we done, he and I. After all, we had arrived late, breathless and a little in love. With what, even we weren't sure. However, our mutual friend probably knows.

Quilt

Not humble, a quilt
takes credit for in-
venting cinema. Jump
cuts? Sure—look:
two shepherdesses

evading rockets. And
here's rose-filled toile-
land again. Other
quilts at the bottom
of the full linen chest

running away from bad
shepherds in toile-land
flip adjacent squares:
stars & elephants.
Some cloth taxis brag

they devised city
planning & graph
paper. The suffocat-
ing chest weeps for
the loss of its only key.

Recipe

Everything in this place will outlive me.
—Anna Akhmatova

A moment: when bread dough, ball-formed with greased hands, rests to rise, it exhibits what seems possible in the stone—expansion into space like a star exploding into the full spheroidal grandeur of a self-luminous celestial body. But the stone can grow only smaller and smaller, eroding, accruing more authority the more needlesome it gets. Abrading fantasy-traps of an ideal past, sometimes the path-bound stone whispers our own noxious monologues to us: *I once young and beautiful, my grandmother a princess, her father courageous, our vast estates filled with people who served us, suffering absence, more absence.* Unless it secret-agents into a shoe, the stone mostly goes unheard, but when successful, we crave the relief denied all those others.

Sontag Diary

[   ] didn't answer. I kept trying. That house: beautiful disordering. Bitter: smoking. Selfish: loving. Lack of whole-heartedness: great failing. I will be all right by this morning. It's entirely safe to risk nothing but therefore bad: entirely boring. [   ] thinks one thing isn't any thing. I think many things might be anythings. I was but am no longer nothing. I don't believe a word I'm saying.

Spaceship

Where shall things hide my I?

When I wake up, I still have one foot in the spaceship. The recycled interior atmosphere of air travel smells like this morning's breath. Outside Vermont is pinetreeing and chipmunking, and the Foxton terrier at the foot of the bed doesn't even sense my return. Strange because I must be covered in extraordinary space dust. Can't she smell those odd ions? Maybe the evidence of my journey will have nothing to do with me. Instead my loved ones will show marks, and I'll be the same as yesterday and every morning. Maybe I've been abducted before, maybe every night. The happiness I always expect to feel and never have—I'm forced to leave on another planet. O! my brothers and sisters of *National Enquirer* cover stories! My dreams are filled with our lives. Will our psychiatrists ever believe we can be happy? I'd like to think joy could be smuggled back, that we're on the brink of waking up one morning without sorrow. My covert prayer: *Maybe tomorrow.*

Spoon

The spoon's unnatural attraction to eyeballs makes it the equal of knives and forks when cutlery's weaponized. You can't trust it. Often this servant thinks about murder while burdened with the task of delivering crème brûlée to a mouth that endlessly wants more. And the tongue—nothing disgusts the spoon more than the tongue licking the smooth parabolic beauty of its bottom like a gluey barnacle single-eye-searching for the best place to encrust, proteinaceous cement glands at the ready, securing a launch site for the barnacle's prosciformed penis to stretch eight, nine times the length of the creature itself, winning the animal kingdom's relative-to-body-size-longest-penis competition, length statistics curling back and forth in sweeping ocean currents. And there comes a day for all human children to question parental wave-hello-or-goodbye commands, small eddies of air in our hotter and hotter atmosphere suspended for a moment. But the air itself knows it hasn't really paused, because cessation doesn't even exist. At some point every single atom in the universe surrenders.

Spring

Bears are breaking into houses again. The season of wakefulness follows winter around like a mother suggesting pink dresses to a teenager's cave-dwelling eyes. Light moves on. Caravaggio painted light's portrait so beautifully, shadow felt adored too. Poison, suppurating wounds, and sunstroke killed him. Light moves on. The bears are always hungry.

Stain

The seep and clot of it. The furtive fingers of it. The blob and spread of it. The orgy of it. The impossible to remove of it. The stand-in for something else of it.

Stamp

WITHDRAWN : and a book leaves the library like a small spaceship flying away from Earth, its one inhabitant barking and barking, his last bone still floating somewhere now.

Starling

Wait a long time for a ticket wait a long time for departure your
dress a stain lie down on the floor listen to feet thudding past
your head a lullaby a thuddaby let the airport's flight architecture
float your dreams of arrayed wings out the enormous window
be awakened by a starling this terminal-trapped bird's going to
fly until it dies not you you'll walk there

Subtle Horror Movies

Monster

An immense lizard standing on two legs does not devour the city. The creature nibbles on it at night, while we are sleeping, but we never notice.

Pathogen

Some of us are not immune. We cough and sweat. Our hero is immune. To what, we do not know.

Visitor From Outer Space

We argue about the existence of God. Evidence for both sides: a church that fills with prayer only when empty.

Suitcase

I hear it whispering, *Can't wait to leave.*

Taxidermy

Glass-domed on a mantle, a rose-headed, pert-beaked finger puppet finch plans the epitaph for its invisible tombstone: *The forest ghettoes trees.*

Teacup

Consider the woman from Des Moines who wakes up after a car accident with a British accent. Empire had been lingering inside her, waiting for some typical violence to let itself out. A silly woman before, now she is also interested in maritime battle strategies. Her stays in the bathtub have been extended. The neighbors hear her yelling about world domination but pay no attention. Because what can the woman do—go to sea in a porcelain teacup? Besides, Des Moines's not a port city.

Tennis Court

On a clay tennis court overgrown with English ivy, a dog the size and color of a roast chicken sits and waits for a clear impulse to be honed into trajectory by a squirrel, chipmunk, rabbit—something small and trying to live. A tennis ball hides in the dark green milderness like a movie star leaving a restaurant through the kitchen.

Test

our soft lead pencils filling in ovals the dulled points darkening
choice after choice

Thermometer

Recalled responses happyen to be notoriously unreliable, said Dr. K after I told him that I had been happy once. He poured a few drops of water through a rough brown sugar cube sitting on a leaf-shaped slotted spoon, until the absinthe in the small glass below clouded as usual. He didn't believe the absinthe had ever been happy either. If I could do things differently, next time I wouldn't sleep with my psychiatrist. Though envisioned responses also happyen to be notoriously unreliable.

Tureen

Like a severed head the tureen sits on a high shelf proclaiming soup, by which it means dreams of oceans. Saline brews from which a cartoon cat could pull a fish skeleton, bones arranged like the locust tree's pinnate leaf or a showgirl's ostrich feather fascinator, the world finding a pleasure and repeating it. Our imitations not as beguiling, the roofed TV antenna, the tension pole shower caddy, the thin louvered bi-fold door to the broom closet always drifting away from its magnet, always angling out into a space that ignores it, a space concentrated on the featured door that permits egress. A dog walks through that doorway, having abandoned a stuffed animal and disembowelment practice. A man walks through that doorway, stunned to be told his five-year-long post-nasal drip has actually been diminishing brain leaking out via nose. The tureen says to itself, *ocean ocean ocean*.

Unused Ashtray

So you and these other people will die of something besides lung cancer. But remember that moment after you'd been introduced to him and he reached over to take a drag of your cigarette without asking? The wingback chair you were sitting in upholstered with deep yellow velvet like woven pollen. The white shirt under his suit coat waving surrender. All the thin dogs and chickens scattering in the streets of your heart as you limousined a bed through the dust. Remember throwing everything away over and over? And the flawless abyss just before hope flared.

Vacation

The sameness of hotel rooms always different. Water glasses wrapped in plastic but not the ghosts—tryst ghosts, press junket ghosts, end-of-business and funeral ghosts—even the ghosts of plastic wrapping unplasticwrapped. The hotel room foregrounds nakedness like a beaker bubbling above a flame signals volatility held in check momentarily. If the television's on but muted, closed captioning describes the world within the world, relying on stenographers rather than cartographers. When producers stint on stenography skill, an inexpensive ear makes *I love you* into *gloved universe*, and *you didn't call* into *din and calamity*. And now in the TV's silence a telephone rings and rings in a movie's hotel room, the phone waiting for someone to answer so the stenographer can type: *The giraffe has a soul but doesn't know it* instead of the main character's actual line: *I've laughed at hazard control dozens of times.* The phone laughs too, until finally a maid answers, precipitating the film's conclusion: *Remember!*

cries the hero, but the stenographer gets it wrong—though we all get that one wrong. The hero can prove one zooed giraffe does know its own soul, but through the stenographer's mishearing fingers, when the maid takes a message, she writes, *The gloved universe is only an ember, a fading enchantment seen as a bright fire by our primitive reverie. Please return this call.*

Weather

*...a longing which is always there
and is never appeased by any object in this world.*
—SIMONE WEIL

When fades fluorescent poster ink and particles loosed up swim the in sky and maybe neon a few fragments past it make the barrier that perfection keeps away from us.

When pouring your milk hand from small a pitcher shaped cow a like shakes and when circles water a glass counter in on the inside itself as the wheeze starts to fridge.

When happening everything is the ongoingness in of when I and don't to stop want I can't that because and anyway the whenness—dust all bits the and and and of and and and the skin pieces hair stars rain faded things things

broken—will break. When then razed quiet in I horizon myself next to myself. Then. No thing. That's I all along what wanted.

Wedding Ring

The void is important.
—Rei Kawakubo

Find a curve uniting body and mouth, Announce you are staying, Then disappear. Warmth persists for a long time in ashes.

X _____

Greedy, the line owns all the world's buildings, every car, and most promises. The line wears its x like a crown and would have no trouble facilitating a treaty or beheading, as long as the space hovering above its uncompromising spine were marked with ink, like a stucco wall red-slashed with graffiti claiming: *This wax-ball's mine*. More than anything the straight-edged signature line likes to dream about its next mate—how curly or jagged, sinuous or spiked—and all the points of entwined contact. The line tells itself these intersections shimmer *love-stars in a forever-sky*. What a romantic, thinks the line's newest autograph, captured on a coerced confession. But what if the line's right and all the moments of our crosscrissings radiate perpetually? What if everything ends in light?

Yellow

A champagne bubble sends a postcard from the yellowniverse: *Dear Firmament, Soon, my love, I will leave the wall of this goblet to join thee—me small, you all the grandeur of the blueniverse. So soon the voyage! Ever since the vintner corked that bottle in which I waited and waited, I've wondered, Am I the astronaut or the spaceship? There's been so much pressure to get the answer right. Now I know. I'll tell you when we're together. Just you and me, Beloved. Kisses.* Oops. The firmament hasn't had the heart to tell the bubble about the vast polyamory it's about to enter into. Nor the time—every millisecond every milliwhere so many weddings.

Zoo

Neither attic nor cellar, though hoarding multitudes, the zoo compares itself to a neighboring apartment building—*that grasping crate-stack*—and spreads out horizontally, offering its animal wares like a junkie selling stolen cassette tapes on a sidewalked blanket. At the entrance, simultaneously mouth and anus, raucous bipeds pay to see themselves costumed in feathers, scales, fur. The zoo tries to love visitors as much as residents but fails each time someone throws a candy wrapper on the ground. Truth is, the zoo doesn't like its work and would prefer to let all the captives go. Looking down on the zoo's pain, the apartment building reckons that seeing the horizon's better than being the horizon—almost optimal evidence: its silver sheath dress sparkling in the sun. Looking up at the building's tall glamour, the zoo pictures a menagerie distributed among the apartments, lions situating themselves in the penthouse, ostriches unfairly relegated to maids' rooms throughout the structure, beasts sullying the pristine with every smear of feces and ear-needling screech. In the zoo's vision, its own now-untenanted cages will house nothing, and the nothing will live joyfully, free to leave at any time.

Landon Godfrey is the author of *Second-Skin Rhinestone-Spangled Nude Soufflé Chiffon Gown* (Cider Press Review), selected by David St. John for the Cider Press Book Award, and two limited-edition letterpress chapbooks, *In the Stone* and *Spaceship*. She has received fellowships from the National Endowment for the Arts and the North Carolina Arts Council. Born and raised in Washington, DC, she now lives in Black Mountain, North Carolina.